Body Language

*Effective Non-verbal Communication
to Understand People, Influence
People and Attract People Instantly*

The information herein is offered for informational purposes solely, and is universal as so. The presentation of the information is without contract or any type of guarantee assurance.

The trademarks that are used are without any consent, and the publication of the trademark is without permission or backing by the trademark owner. All trademarks and brands within this book are for clarifying purposes only and are the owned by the owners themselves, not affiliated with this document.

Table of Contents

Introduction

I will like to congratulate and thank you for downloading this book. This book provides proven steps and strategies on how to connect instantly with anyone using non-verbal body language.

Have you ever wished that you have that desirable charisma and absolute powerful presence without saying a word? Or do you feel that there is something missing in your communication when you are speaking to people? Or have you ever wanted to be the person who walks into a room of strangers and yet capable of capturing everyone's attention instantly?

This self-help guide aims to assist you to implement such impactful social-psychological techniques so as to understand exactly what others are thinking without any words.

Anyone would love to decipher how a person may be feeling by 'reading' him or her. There are numerous TV series, Like Lie to Me and House that show you how tiny movements of your body or certain personality traits reveal numerous secrets about a person. Cal Lightman in Lie to Me tries to identify who the criminal is by looking at the smallest movements that the person makes. Sir Arthur Conan Doyle wrote how Sherlock Holmes could tell a person's profession just through his handshake.

Every person in the world gives away his or her inner thoughts almost every second of every day. You will be able to read a person too when you understand the science behind reading this unspoken language. You are probably wondering whether it is psychology that you will need to learn in order to understand this language. Well, the answer here is no.

The language of the body is something that comes in naturally and we use the language to pass signals. All you need to do is learn to pick up these signals by paying attention to what each signal means. Learning a few words of the language too, with just a little practice, will help you read people in a way you may never have before.

You will certainly be amazed at what you were missing after understanding the nonverbal communication.

Chapter 1:
The Origins of Body Language

Body language is very essential when it comes to communication. It is a tool that one can use to crack deals in business or to understand the people around them. This chapter talks about the origins of Body language which is essential to know in order to understand the importance of body language.

The Origins of Body Language

What do we know about the roots of body language? Do you think it is something that we are born with or something we learn?

It is difficult to answer this question and there are two reasons behind this:

- Body language is a tool or an art that has evolved over time to aid human beings meet their social needs. There are numerous anthropologists and scientists who study different kinds of gestures to try and understand if these have developed over time and the purpose behind why they have developed. Most of these gestures have been known to match those of primates. Primates use certain gestures to communicate with each other which have become prominent in human beings too.

- When body language is used as a mode of communication, it can be categorized into several groups – inborn and developed. Some gestures are inborn and are used by people from different parts of the world while conversing with the people around them. There are other gestures that have been developed on observing the people from different cultures. The latter are only used often when practiced over time.

Therefore, it all depends on the person. You are not taught on how to scowl with anger or laugh. Your brain has been programmed to react in a certain manner when you are angry or happy. However, you can choose to change the way you laugh or the way you react when you find another gesture more appealing to you. You may have also learned how to stand and portray yourself as a confident person and project a positive image. If not, you will be able to grasp a good idea on the different ways you can do this over the course of the book.

Do we still need body language?

You may be wondering why we need to use body language when we have words to help get our message across to the people around you. You may be wondering whether you can communicate with the people around you without having to use body language.

The first thing to remember is that human beings have only recently started communicating using speech. There is a lot of speculation on when it is that we started to speak. Although we have been speaking for over thousands of years, we are relatively new to speech. Prior to this time, we used gestures and signals (non - verbal cues) like animals to communicate our thoughts across to someone.

You may have heard the saying; "Old habits die hard" which is true in this case as well. Body language still plays an important role in our communication, whether or not we choose to accept it. You will be able to notice this when you look at someone who is talking over the phone. Although the person on the line will not be able to look at them, they do wave their hands around and make certain expressions when speaking.

This may seem very primitive when you think about it. But, in the days when we did not know how to speak, we only used grunting sounds and our hands to put our point across. Yes, we did not look really good while making these sounds or performing these actions, but we did get our point across. We were able to tell our fellow humans that we wanted to go hunting at that particular time.

You will never be able to communicate effectively if you do not use body language when you are talking to someone. This implies that verbal and non – verbal communication go hand – in hand. You should consider body language to be the seasoning to your food. You can make your food taste differently by adding different dressings to it. In the very same way, you will be able to say something and imply it differently using body language. For instance, you can say "I am okay" using different gestures and signs which would give the receiver different meanings.

The Study of Body Language

The study of body language began with the actors when they starred in Silent Films. The actors, like Charlie Chaplin, had to learn how to express their attitude, emotions and their status using body language and they were extremely good at doing that! The amazing thing about the silent films was that we were able to decipher what the actors were trying to say even when they lacked a voice. This is proof that body language can tell so much about what a person thinks and feels.

Who was the first to study body language and its origin?

Charles Darwin, the father of evolution, was the first to study body language and its origin. He studied the body language of animals and human beings and tried to understand the similarities between the two. He has made a note of all his research in his book, "The Expression of the Emotions in Man and Animals" in the year 1872.

He made careful observations and identified that human beings, like animals, do share certain inborn behavior that are common in every human being irrespective of race or region. These cues, which were non – verbal, helped in revealing certain emotions which helped us communicate with other human beings.in the book, mentioned above, Charles Darwin has established the fact that there is a science behind body language. This has been the base of many researches that have been conducted on body language.

The major chunk of research on body language began in the late 1960s which is a little surprising since it exists since the beginning of time. Since the late 1960s, it has become an essential part of many subjects – psychiatry, anthropology, social sciences and even business.

Now that you have understood the essence of body language and also read a little about the history of body language, let us move into understanding certain aspects of body language.

Chapter 2:
Body Language Does Matter

When you understand the basics of body language and also the silent conversation, you will be able to go a long way in life. This is similar to understanding what a person's attire says about them and also understanding what your clothes are saying.

A person with an understanding on the language and who also pays attention to how he can present himself, he will be able to express himself the way he wants to and also understand what people around him want from him. This guide on body language focuses on two crucial aspects:

1. How to control your reactions to always say what it is that you want to say

2. How to understand another person's body to analyze what they are feeling and thinking

To understand this, you do not need to be a spy, detective or a professional gambler. You can take advantage of the above points just by understanding what your body can say. When you are able to see and understand what another person's reaction is towards you, you will be able to understand what they think about you which will make it easier to understand the kind of people who you would want to do business with. The first aspect to consider is based on practicality. You will be able to train yourself to stop undermining yourself. You will be able to move with a greater level of confidence while grabbing the attention of the people around you. This would lead to a cause and loop effect; for instance, when you see a person standing and always moving around like a confident leader, the people around him start thinking of him as a leader – which would lead to him considering himself a leader.

Does this work?

Everybody actually thinks this at least once. They probably think that this is too good to be true, which would be the case till they understand the intricacies of body language. Would you be able to understand whether a person is flirting, in love, sick or lying when you look at their eyes or their hands? Would you be able to get more tips, close a deal, scare off an attacker or reassure a person you love easily when you shift your posture?

Well, this is true, albeit conditionally. A person who is trained also will not be able to always have a perfect reading score. This is for the reason that con men and liars are experienced with body language and will be making an effort to control all their movements and their gestures to avoid giving their lie or con away.

In numerous cases, intuition is as necessary as training in understanding body language. There are a lot of non – verbal cues that occur in seconds that would make it extremely difficult to understand what the person is trying to say. The only way you would be able to process these cues would be to re – watch the complete exchange in a slow motion. Since we do not have that luxury, we will need to count on our gut and notice and analyze the cues to help us get a feel of the situation.

With all that being said, you can gain a lot of information that you can gain when you understand and analyze the body language of the person talking to you. When you control your own posture and gestures, you will be able to influence people around you irrespective of whether or not they are aware of what it is that you are doing. This is because most reactions are hardwired into the human brain. All in all, it is a yes – all of this really works. You will not be wasting your time by reading this.

How hard must I think about this?

This is a slightly difficult question. This is because you will need to pay attention and a good amount of it. But, this does not mean that you will need to watch people's frantic movements and try to remember them since you will not be able to gain anything out of it. This is because you will be distracted and will also be less effective at non – verbal and verbal communication – which would lead to you missing the whole point of the conversation.

You will be able to learn better when you begin to practice in situations that are controlled. All you need to do is use certain moments in your life where you do not have to be under too much pressure – like shopping in the grocery store or when you are at the movies or at a restaurant – to observe the way other people behave. You will need to read their gestures, stances and their facial expressions.

You can also practice when you are at parks, stores, public streets and certain areas that have an exposure to the public. All you need to do is practice when your social life or your business is never on the line. You will be shocked to see how you find certain basics of body language materialize.

You will not become Sherlock Holmes or Dr. Gregory House, but you will be able to lose the thought where you believe that a person opening his palms to you would be asking you to trust him. You will be able to understand the different signs better and react to the situation in the right way.

Things are not what they always seem

It is simple to understand what is happening in a conversation – it is not easy, just very simple. You will need to be able to match what you are seeing and hearing in your surroundings where the entire conversation is happening through which you will be able to draw all possible conclusions. A lot of people always see things that they assume they are seeing or they think they are seeing. Let us look at a story to demonstrate this:

While walking through the woods, two people come across a deep hole.

A: "Well, that hole looks really deep."

B: "Let us toss a few pebbles into the hole and assess how deep the hole is."

The two of them throw a few pebbles into the hole and wait, but there is absolutely no sound.

A: "That is an extremely deep hole; we may not have heard the sound for this very reason. Let us throw in a bigger pebble into the hole to hear a noise."

They pick up two rocks that are the size of a football and throw them into the hole. They wait, but could not hear anything.

B: "There seems to be a railway keeper in the weeds here. If we toss that into the hole, we will be able to hear a definitive noise."

The two of them drag the railway sleeper towards the hole and heave it into it –but alas, no sound was heard. A goat appeared out of nowhere from the woods and ran towards the two men. It runs right in between the two of them going as fast as it actually could.

The goat then leaped into the air and disappeared right into the hole. The men stand aside and are bewildered by what they have seen. A farmer comes right out of the woods and asks the two men if they saw his goat come out of the woods. The two men are surprised and say that they did see the goat and saw that it jumped right into the hole. The farmer says that that could not be his goat since his goat was tied to a railway sleeper.

How well do you know your hand?

There are times when we say that we know things like we know the back of our hands. Numerous experiments prove otherwise – it was concluded that less than 5% of the people can identify the back of their very own hands using a photograph. There were numerous experiments conducted, especially on television programs which show that people in general are not good at reading and interpreting the signals of body language.

One experiment was where a large mirror was set at the end of a lobby which gave the people the illusion that they were standing in a very long corridor – one that went through the hotel and out at the back of the lobby. Large plants were hung at the beginning of the corridor which made it look like there was another person entering the lobby. The person entering after the first would not be recognizable since their face would be covered with the plants. People in the front would only be able to see the person behind them from below their neck.

The guest in front observed the guest at the back only for five seconds and would need to turn towards the reception desk. But, when they were asked whether they were able to recognize the person in front of them, 85% of the men were not able to recognize the other guest. There were a few men who were unable to recognize themselves in the mirror! But, there were 58% women who understood that the thing behind them was a mirror, and close to 30% of them were able to state that the guest behind them looked very familiar.

How do you spot body language contradictions?

There are people everywhere who are trying to understand the body language of the politicians since people everywhere know that the politicians often pretend to believe in certain things they do not believe in. These people also begin to infer that these politicians are in fact not who they claim to be.

Politicians spend a great deal of time lying, pretending, avoiding, dodging, ducking, hiding their emotions and feelings and using smoke screens to wave to their friends, who are imaginary, in the crowd. But, we know that they will definitely slip up by contradicting what they are trying to say through their body language and it is because of this that we watch them with utmost concentration. We want to catch them at their game!

How will the book help you?

Body language is an essential part of communication. Through the different chapters in the book, you will be able to grasp the essence of body language and how you can use it to leave a positive impression on the people you meet. There are different techniques given in the chapters which explain how you must carry yourself if you want to be perceived as someone who is confident.

You will learn about posture and stance and how you should never invade someone's personal space. The way you shake your hand or the way you place your hands while conversing with someone says a lot about you. Over the course of the book, you will be able to understand these aspects with greater detail.

Chapter 3:
Basics of body language

We all know someone who can walk into a room that is full of people and will be able to give you an accurate description of the people in the room and also their relationships. That person will also be able to tell you how the people in the room are feeling. The original way of communication, before language even evolved, between human beings was by reading a person's attitude and thoughts through their behavior.

Most communication was always done through writing in books, newspapers and letters and this was before the radio came into the picture. It was because of this that people who are poor orators were successful in those times because they were able to write well. When the radio was invented, people who were good orators were able to grasp a good command over the people around them – people like Winston Churchill was great at this since he spoke wonderfully. He would have been unable to do this in this generation since people assess another person based on their looks.

People these days understand that it is always about a person's image and appearance. Politicians and other famous people have grasped this and have professionals train them to come across as caring, sincere and honest even when they are not!

It is incredible that body language has been studied for a long time, but it has only been actively studied since the 1960s. People still believe that speech is the main form of communication. Speech has only recently become a part of our communication and it was only used to convey certain data and facts. It was only 2 million or 500,000 years ago that speech was developed which was when the human brain's size tripled. Before that, it was only through sounds and body language that people conveyed their emotions and feelings which is what the case is. Since most people focus only on what they say, they are uninformed of the importance of body language.

The spoken language helps you understand how important body language actually is. Let us look at a few phrases which show the importance of body language is:

1. Keep a stiff upper lip

2. Keep your chin up

3. Stay in a distance of arm's length

4. Get it off your chest

5. Kiss my ass

6. Face up to it

7. Put your best foot forward

A few of these phrases are difficult to digest and you may not really trust in them, but there are a few that are eye – openers. There are a few more phrases that can keep coming up, but you would either buckle at reading these phrases or you turn off from the idea of body language completely. I hope that these phrases did not set you off but helped to motivate you.

Why is it never what you say?

Although we need to look at a person's eyes when we first look at them, we always make a decision, and a very fast one at that, about their dominance, friendliness, potential as a partner and so on and so forth either from up close or from afar.

Numerous researchers agree that verbal communication is often used only to convey information whereas body language is utilized to negotiate interpersonal attitudes and sometimes used as a substitute for verbal communication. For instance, a woman can give another woman a look that actually kills, which would convey the meaning clearly. This could be done without the woman even saying a word.

There are numerous people who find it very difficult to accept that human beings are still animals – biologically speaking. Charles Darwin has said that human beings are a species of primates that have learned to walk and talk – basically primates with an advanced brain. But, like every other species we are dominated by rules that control our reactions, actions, gestures and body language. The most fascinating thing is that human beings are aware of their postures, movements and gestures. They are also aware that these could be telling an entirely different story.

How does body language reveal thoughts and emotions

Body language is a way by which you represent your emotional conditions. Every movement and gesture can be used as a valuable key to assess a person's emotions and feelings at that very second. For instance, a person who is self – conscious about gaining weight may tug at the fold of the skin that is under his chin; a woman who is acutely aware of the extra weight on her thighs may keep smoothing her dress; a person who is defensive or fearful may always cross his legs and his arms while a man talking with a woman who has large breasts would be unable to converse with the woman without looking at her breasts and would constantly make groping gestures with his hands.

The most important thing about reading body language is to be able to understand any person's emotional conditions while paying attention to what it is they are saying and making note of the conditions in which they are saying what they are saying. This would give you the power to separate reality from fantasy and fact from fiction.

In recent times, we have started to give speech an extremely high level of importance since we have started to enhance our ability to be conversationalists. We have become unaware of the fact that our body can speak a thousand words and that each word spoken by your posture and gesture has a great impact. This is the case although we do acknowledge the fact that a majority of the messages in a face – to – face conversation are always revealed through certain signals by your body.

Women are more perceptive

When we label certain people as intuitive or perceptive, we are referring – knowingly or unknowingly – to their ability to read and interpret a person's body language. These people are able to separate and compare body language and verbal signals. There may have been times when you may have had a 'feeling' that a person is lying to you. This could be because of the fact that you were able to separate the person's body language from his spoken words; it also means that the two of them do not add up for you. This is what speakers refer to as audience awareness.

For instance, if there is an audience that has begun to slouch in their seats with their chins pressed towards their chest and their arms crossed protectively over their chest, the speaker (if intuitive) must be able to grasp the fact that his delivery did not go across well and will need to react fast to avoid losing the audience completely. If the speaker was not perceptive or intuitive, he will continue to make the same blunder no matter what the body language of the audience says.

It is on record that women are more perceptive than men because of which the term 'women's intuition' came into existence. Women have an ability that is innate to decipher and pick up non – verbal signals and have a very good eye for small details. It is for this very reason that very few husbands can lie to their wives and get away with it and conversely, women can pull a fast one over their husbands without them even realizing it.

Psychologists at Harvard University were able to conduct research on how women are more alert towards body language when compared to men. They conducted the experiment by showing short films with the audio turned off. The film showed a man and woman talking to each other and the participants in the room were asked to decipher what was being said by the actors on the screen just by looking at their expressions. The results showed that women were able to read the situation 87% of the time and accurately while men were only able to do so 47% of the time. Men who were in occupations that could be categorized into nurturing – acting, nursing, creative directors and so on – were able to do as good as women. Gay men were also able to score well irrespective of their occupation.

Female intuition is profoundly evident in women who have given birth and raised children. This is because the mother relies solely on the non – verbal communication that happens between the baby and her. It is for this very reason that women are more perceptive than men since they begin to read signals right from the start.

Culturally Learned, Genetic or Inborn

When you cross your legs, do you cross your left leg over your right or your right leg over your left? When you cross your arms across your chest, do you cross your right arm over your left or your left arm over your right?

Many people are not able to describe what they do to utmost perfection until they do it. Cross your arms across your chest now and then try to reverse the order of arms quickly. Which way feels better to you? Is there a particular way that feels completely incorrect? Evidence does suggest that this could be a genetic gesture and for this very reason cannot be changed as easily as one would want.

Countless research and debates have been conducted to decipher if non – verbal signals were indeed genetically transferred, inborn or learned in one way or another. There has been evidence collected from the blind that would not have been able to learn the art of non – verbal communication through any visual channel. The body language and gestures of people from different cultures from across the world was compared with our ancestors, or nearest relatives (anthropologically speaking), apes.

The conclusion of this research has indicated that certain gestures fall under each of the categories mentioned. For instance, a baby is born with the ability to suck and this ability could be either genetic or inborn. A German scientist Eibl-Eibesfeldt concluded that children were able to smile irrespective of whether they were born blind or deaf and this goes to say that the art of smiling could also be an inborn gesture. Friesen, Sorenson and Ekman studied the facial expressions of certain people from five widely distinct and different cultures. Their conclusions supported certain beliefs that Darwin had about inborn gestures. They were able to identify that every culture used a few basic facial gestures to show certain emotions leading them to believe that these gestures were inborn.

There is a lot of debate that still exists when it comes to identifying whether certain gestures are learned culturally or whether they are genetic. For instance, a majority of men put their coat on by putting their right arm in first while women always put their left arm in first. This example shows that women use the right hemisphere of their brain to perform this action while men use the left hemisphere of their brain.

Another example you could consider would be − a man when walking down a crowded street would always turn his body towards a woman who is passing by him whereas a woman would turn her body away from him in order to protect her breasts. Would you think this is an inborn gesture or do you think the woman would have picked this up from observing women around her?

Chapter 4:
Understanding Personal Space

Every animal always marks its territories using certain mechanisms. A territory is a space or an area that is around a person which he claims is his own; it is like an extension of his own body. There is a defined air space that exists around the person's body which is his own territory. This chapter deals with that defined air space and how one will react when this space is invaded.

A person's personal space is dependent on the population of the country or area he grew up in. therefore, it is safe to say that the personal space is culturally defined. Some cultures would not mind a person standing very close to them while there are others where this is condemned.

There are four distinct zones that a person has around them. Let us discuss these zones in a little detail to understand how we must never invade a person's personal space.

Intimate Zone

This is an extremely important zone and is between 6 – 8 inches from the body. This is the zone that the person guards as if it were his own property. It is only the people that we are close with who are allowed into this zone. There is a sub zone that is extended up to 6 inches which is a zone that can be entered only during physical contact which is intimate.

Personal Zone

This zone is between 18 and 48 inches from a person's body. It is the distance at which a person stands from others at business parties, social functions and gatherings.

Social Zone

This is the zone that extends from a person's body to 4 or 12 feet. A person would stand at this distance from a stranger – the carpenter or plumber working at home, new employees at work and any other person he may not know well.

Public Zone

This zone extends over 12 feet from a person's body. When you address a large group, you will find yourself in a comfortable situation when you choose to stand at this distance.

These distances would decrease between women and increase between men.

How to Use the Zones for a Positive Approach

The intimate zone is often entered by people for two reasons only:

1. The person is a friend or a close relative or the person is making a sexual advance

2. The person is ready to attack

It may be okay for a person to intrude on another person's personal and social zones, but if he intrudes the Intimate Zone, there will definitely be certain physiological changes that take place in the body. Your heart will begin to pump blood faster, which results in adrenaline being pumped into the bloodstream thereby getting your body ready to fight if needed.

When you meet a person for the first time and you put your arm, in a friendly way, that person may begin to feel negative towards you since you have invaded his intimate zone. They may smile and try to appear friendly, but they do not want your arm around them.

If you want people around you to feel comfortable, you will need to remember the golden rule: "Keep your distance."

The more intimate your relationship is with a person, the more you have the chance to move closer to that person. For instance, a new employee may feel that the people around him are cold towards him. But, the only thing that the people are doing is place him in the Social Zone till they know him better. When they get to know him better he will move between the zones and would sometimes even make it to a person's intimate zone.

Chapter 5:
Stance and Posture

Gestures made by a person's hands are small and the movements of the eyes are minute and would need you to be up close to see them. But, a person's stance can always be read and understood from a distance.

The way a person stands or moves their limbs come from our primate ancestors. Human beings share most of their gestures with their ape relatives. Posture and stance are related to the feelings of survival – stress, aggressiveness, defensiveness and dominance.

Dominant Stance

You have to keep it in mind that dominance and aggression are different things. A person who feels in charge and secure is very different from a person who is looking for a fight.

- A person who is dominant would stand in a pose that is open and squared off. He will fearlessly expose his vulnerable vitals – like his stomach

- The dominant person would spread his legs close to shoulder – width apart

- He would stand with chin thrusted forward and his head raised high, while exposing his neck

- His arms will hang comfortably on the sides or he would clasp his hands behind his back. He would never place his hands in front of his body since that would definitely indicate defensiveness

- The people he is interacting with face him. People would not turn to see him with a sideways glace, they would turn to face him with their whole body.

- When he is seated, he would place his feet slightly apart and spread his legs (this is an instinctive gesture which would expose the pelvic region)

- His hands are placed on the table, slightly apart from each other instead of interlacing them in front of his body.

As is obvious, a person who is dominant will be able to give a sense of openness. He will be able to show the front of his body without any fear. He will be able to say, "I am here and I do not fear you" just by the way he stands. A policeman, politician or any leader will always use this stance. This is a good stance to train yourself to get used to since it will help in giving people the impression that you are a leader and you will be able to inspire respect in the people around you.

Aggressive Stance

A person who is aggressive is not a person in control – it is a person who would like to be in control. The stance that this kind of person would have is potentially violent and portrays a challenge. You will need to keep a keen eye on this kind of behavior. These people are not thinking of doing anything violent but they are gearing up for a fight. You will need to calm this person down before you start to deal with them in a rational manner,

- The person will probably put all his weight on the foot that is in front as if he is crouching to spring

- The legs are placed close to each other with the dominant leg a little ahead of the other leg. This is to prepare their muscles to spring into action if necessary.

- The head is tilted forward and the chin is lowered to protect the neck from any harm. This could be interpreted as a sign of weakness and the person would try to shift his torso upward in order to take up the receiver's personal space.

- The arms of the person are raised towards other people – aggressive gestures like pointing fingers at them are often made along with emphatic gestures.

- The person will have his hands up in front of him in the same way he would if he were to be boxing. The body is turned slightly to ensure that one shoulder guards he center of his body to avoid exposing any vitals.

- If the person is seated, he would lean forward with his palms facing downward on the table. This would look like the person is trying to ensure that he has the space to leap out of the seat if necessary.

You will see these postures in salesmen, stock brokers, lawyers, political aides and certain people who are looking for an argument. If you are conscious of the fact that you are adopting an aggressive stance, you will need to try to shift into the dominant stance since it is more centered. It is always good to look like someone who is in control as opposed to a person who feels like he needs to fight for control.

Defensive Stance

It is simple to spot a person who is never at ease. Their body will send out micro signals and gestures which would indicate that they are trying to protect their body and cover it as much as possible. A person who is standing in this way would most likely be feeling bad about something. They could be intimidated by their situation or are always looking at themselves in a way that says that they are at a disadvantage. If this is not the case, they could be concealing something important and are worried about getting caught in the act.

- The weight of the person's body will be leaning away from the people he is conversing with. It would be pointed in the direction of an escape.

- His shoulders would be raised and the chin would be placed close to the chest in order to protect his neck

- His arms would cover the front of his body which would often mean that the person would have his hands clasped together across the chest or crossed over in front of the pelvic region.

- If the person is sitting down, his arms would be held close to his body. He would lean on his elbows or would cross his arms in front of him on the tabletop.

A person who has this stance is showing signs of worry and will need to be calmed down. It is always good to give them their personal space and to always make gestures that will soothe the person down. Try to choose calming words along with the gestures to make a profound effect on the person. If you find yourself folding your arms in front of you to protect your torso, you should understand that something is making you uncomfortable and you need to identify a way to correct that. You will also need to move into the position of the dominant stance to ensure that you exude confidence.

Mixed Signals

Most often you will find people exhibiting more than one of the traits at the same time. You will need to look for other signals of body language along with the posture cues - observe the movement of the eyes and the gestures.

In most cases, feet and arms will be the best indicators as opposed to a torso. People have been told to stand straight very often and always artificially yank themselves upright irrespective of whether they are nervous or angry. If the person's arms are folded defensively with the feet pointing towards an exit route, or if the person is shifting on his legs as if he is ready to lunge, you will know that the stance is not heartfelt.

Chapter 6:
Hand Gestures

There is an old joke that say, "If you want to close an Italian's shop, you need to just tie his hands behind his back."

Italians are known to use their hands a lot while they are talking. People across the world may not do it as much as the Italians but they do use their hands while trying to make conversation. The way you position your hand is not culturally trained the way a straight backed posture is which would make it very easy to judge the way a person is feeling.

Open Palm

When you are looking at a person, you will need to pay close attention to their palms. If you are able to see the person's palms, it will be able to tell you a lot about what they are thinking. When the palms are kept open, it shows that the person is not holding a weapon and is not preparing to make a blow. In primates, it is an act of submission but in human beings it is an act of cooperation and willingness to listen. Men and women both show their palms to people they are trying to talk to or make an appeal to.

- Politicians hold their hands raised over the podium and apart from each other. They face their palms towards the audience to invite them to share their thoughts and ideas.

- A celebrity who is seeking public attention would raise his or her arms and wave at the crowds. If the paparazzi are around them and they would want to discourage them from asking too many questions, the celebrities would put their hands inside their pockets or at their sides.

- Magicians and con artists always spread their hands over a table or face their palms towards the crowd to show them that they have nothing hidden in them.

- If a palm is turned upward, it is a signal for panhandlers and beggars. A person with his hand raised would often be asking for assistance. For instance, in a classroom, students who are asking a question would raise their hands over their heads with their palms facing outward.

- A "high five" is a way of celebrating team work and achievement.

- When a person is being questioned by a person with high authority, would often hold his hands up to indicate that he or she is willing to cooperate.

If you find that the people around you are facing their palms outward, they are willing to listen to what you are trying to say. A salesperson would look for this since he would be given an invitation to speak if the palms of the listener are faced outward.

Good presenters and salesmen would often use certain excuses to ensure that people open their hands up. They could hand out brochures or samples which would help in grasping the crowd's attention. You will be able to invite people to listen to your thoughts and opinions using an open palm. If you find that people around you have become hostile, you can use this gesture to calm them down.

Closed Palm

A palm that is facing downward signifies the opposite of the association that one makes when the palm is open or faced upward.

A closed or downward – turned palm signify the readiness to strike or clench and this gesture asserts a certain level of dominance over the person who is being gestured at. The Roman and the Nazi salute are the perfect examples of this gesture – they are designed to indicate power and also the willingness to fight. A subtle variation may occur in a person's body when he or she is looking at controlling or confronting someone.

- Bosses, coaches and people who give instructions often use this gesture while barking orders. They usually extend one hand forward with their palms facing downward while making chop like motions to emphasize the points they are making.

- Knocking the pulpit or the podium with their hand down and their fists closed is a gesture that is typical in people who consider themselves the authority. They believe that they are to direct their audience as opposed to persuading them.

- When a person is pointing, his palm is faced downward and has the appearance of a closed fist that is ready to punch someone. This makes it an extremely aggressive gesture when it is used in another person's personal space.

- A person showing his thumbs up or down would be passing judgement and would most likely be a dominant.

- The "V" and the raised middle finger are all considered rude gestures since the palm is always faced away from the receiver.

If you find even the slightest gesture where the person you are talking to is moving his palm inward or hiding it, you will need to understand that that person is unable to get along with you. Something as simple as holding the pen with the wrist turned towards the ceiling or interlaced hands under the chin are signs of disinterest – the person could completely disagree with what you are saying or you have lost him in the conversation.

You will need to use palm hiding gestures when there is a need to communicate something urgently and in an authoritative manner. You will need to signal to gain someone's attention without being rude towards them. The best way you can do this is by placing your hands behind your back or putting them in your pockets. Ensure that you do not place your arms across your chest since that indicates a sign of defensiveness and it will make you appear less in control.

Touching the face

If a child says something that is wrong, he or she will immediately clasp his or her hand over the mouth in order to hold the words inside. This is an impulse that stays with us as we grow older. There are other face and head touches which have certain implications which have been listed below:

- If a person is touching his lips often, it is a sign of dishonestly. If not of dishonesty, it is a sign of withholding information or misleading a person. It could be a gesture which can be construed as "I did say something, but parts of it are not entirely right."

- Since our childhood, the back of our heads have been stroked to soothe us. If a person is scratching the back of his head or rubbing it repeatedly, he could be feeling a certain level of agitation on the topic being discussed.

- If a person is supporting his head, he is showing a sign of weariness.

- When the chin or cheek is placed on the hands, it is an indication of boredom or tiredness. It could also mean that the person is not involved with what is going on around him or her.

Facial gestures must often be taken with a pinch of salt. A person who scratches the back of his head either once or more than once fast is probably just trying to get rid of an itch. If the very same person is repeating the gesture many times throughout the conversation, he is demonstrating signs of agitation. You will then need to look for other signs to ensure that you are reading the person correctly.

When it comes to your body language, there is little or no benefit that you will gain by touching your face. If you are apologizing to someone, it is good to place your hand behind your head since that would show a certain level of vulnerability. Always resist the need to touch your lips or place your head in your hands since those send out negative signals.

Chapter 7:
The Handshake

Greeting using a handshake can be dated to as far back as ancient Rome where men would greet each other by clasping onto the other's forearms. It was claimed that this gesture was used to check for any hidden weapons, but there were numerous Roman garments that left the forearms bare. A man could easily hide his weapons in his sleeves if he did indeed need to carry any weapons. The gesture evolved in order to share strength which subtly encouraged the cooperation between people as opposed to any competition.

The modern handshake is based on the same purpose. People use it as a gesture to show signs of cooperation and it is for this very reason that this gesture has become a major part of the initial greeting. It is also used to seal a bargain. When the Western Culture spread across the world, people across the world began to shake hands irrespective of what their culture may be.

Taking Charge

When you want to take charge, you will need to master the dominant handshake. If you read the previous part carefully, you will not be surprised to read that this shake is the one where your palms are tuned downward which would force the other person to face his hand upward to meet your hand. The rest of the body would be in the same fixed position to ensure that the other person cannot escape the role of the submissive.

- Arms are crossed at the center of the person's chest which would make the handshake on the dominant shaker's slightly off hand side. This would turn his palm towards the floor while his wrist is pointing inward.

- The arm is always held stiffly when extended fully and the only way to shake the hand would be to move the shoulders. This would make it difficult to rotate the wrist making it a forceful handshake as opposed to a polite handshake.

- Fingers will need to be held tightly together when the shake is offered. This is an aggressive gesture since the fingers would be tightly pressed together only when the palm is facing downward.

If you do this firmly and not forcefully, it is a handshake that can be used with ease. You do not need to crush the other person's hand and you definitely do not need to move into the other person's space. When you subtly tilt your wrist downward, you will be able to establish a certain level of control.

If you have aggressive body language, you will only be prompting defensive or negative reactions from the other person. If someone were to try and force a dominant handshake on you, you will need to take a step forward and rotate your body either to your right or left, thereby crossing the dominant person's path in your final step. Your elbow will hook around when you make the turn and the other person will need to rotate outward in order to shake your hand. If a person is forcing you to take an upward palm handshake, do not struggle with them visibly. Just use both your hands to shake their hand, that is close the dominant's hand in your dominant hand with your submissive hand below.

Submissive Handshake

When you turn your palm upward (as mentioned earlier) you will be giving the impression that you are open to what is being said. This is a submissive gesture since it would show that you do not have any weapons in your hand and are ready to show trust.

You can use this handshake to ensure that a person who is nervous can be put at ease or show a willingness to follow a person's lead.

- This is an easy handshake since the elbow will rotate outward naturally. You will need to turn your body in order to step to the right of the person's whose hand you are shaking and let your hand swing slightly outside of the center of your mass with your wrist rotated outward slightly.

- You will only need to tilt slightly. You should ensure that you look dignified and that you are not offering a slap on the palm.

- You will need to grip firmly to compensate for the fact that you are using a gesture that signals weakness. You do not need to crush the person's hand but you will need to make sure that your handshake is not limp.

A person who is eager to shake hands this way is not exuding confidence and would probably be feeling too stressed or is unsure of the situation at hand. You will need to give them their personal space in either case and will need to ensure that you keep your body language open and calm.

This is a good shake to offer to a person when you are already at an advantage and you want them to be reassured of the situation they are in. you can also use this shake when you are apologizing to another person. You should avoid this handshake when you are striking a business deal since you will need to give the shaker a good picture of your position in the deal.

Two Handed Shakes

A one handed gesture is usually a good handshake. When you add the second hand, you will be moving into the other person's space and this could seem either aggressive or intimate for most daily purposes.

It is always good to use a two handed handshake when you want to display a special connection that you may have with someone and are also highlighting their importance to you in that moment. This could also be used to establish a level of control on the person whose hand you may be shaking.

The higher you go on the other person's arm, the more intimate you are with that person. when you clasp the wrist of the other person's hand, you are making them feel special (for instance a preacher or a politician would hold another person's hands this way to show them who the boss is and also make them feel special). If you are shaking hands with a family member or a close friend, you can touch the upper arm or the shoulder showing intimacy.

How hard to Shake?

This is a very common question that most people have about shaking hands. How hard do you squeeze another person's hands? Do you squeeze hard enough to feel the pressure in your hands or enough to feel the deeper tissue in your bones? You can also have a brief handshake, which lasts only for the first up and down shake. You can then move into a more neutral grip which would be more inviting.

For instance, hold a small, ripe tomato in your hand. You will need to ensure that you do not squeeze the tomato too hard so as to rupture its skin. This is how hard you need to squeeze while shaking someone's hands.

Make sure that you always keep your handshakes brief. A single up and down shake is authoritative and brisk. When you continue to shake the person's hands, it will feel like you are forcing them to shake your hands.

Chapter 8:
Eye Signals and Facial Expressions

We have always been preoccupied with the effect of eyes on human behavior. When you maintain eye contact, you will be able to regulate a conversation and will also be able to assert a certain level of dominance. We spend a lot of time during face – to – face conversations looking at the other person's face. Therefore, it is essential that you pay attention to eye signals.

When people meet each other for the first time, they make judgments about each other based on what they see. You may have heard phrases like, 'He looks dominant', 'He looks like he can kill', 'She has such pretty eyes' and so on. The eyes are the most revealing and accurate signals of human communication since the pupils work independently of the brain.

Dilated Pupils

In certain conditions, your pupils will contract and dilate depending on your attitude and your mood. The dilation and contraction depends on the change in your mood – negative to positive and vice versa. If someone is very excited, his or her pupils will dilate up to four times the actual size. However, when a person is angry, the pupils will contract and become beady little eyes or snake eyes. A person with lighter eyes is easier to read since the dilation and contraction are visible.

Eyes are a key cue in courtship. Women wear make up on their eyes to emphasize or enhance their eyes. If a man is attracted to a woman, his pupils would definitely dilate and the woman would be able to decode this change in his eyes unconsciously. It is for this reason that most romantic encounters take place in places that are dimly lit since every person's eyes would dilate by a fraction which would create an impression that people are interested in each other.

It will take time for a person to be able to read a person's emotions through their eyes. Practice is what will make you perfect. Ensure that you do not stare into another person's eyes when you are trying to read them. This will definitely scare them off!

Giving a person the eye

Human beings are the only primates to have whites in their eyes as opposed to the complete dark eyes that apes have. The white in the eye evolved to aid in communication since a person would be able to identify where people were looking.

Women are hardwired to read a man's emotions and it is for this reason that women have more white in their eyes when compared to men. It is easier to identify where a woman is looking on account of the whites. Apes do not have too much of white, so their prey do not know that they are being approached by an ape which gives the ape a greater probability of succeeding at hunting.

Eyebrow Flashes

This gesture is one that is used to greet a person who is at a distance from you. this is a gesture that has been used since the ancient times and is a universal gesture. Monkeys and apes use it as a way to greet other apes during a social gathering, which confirms that this is an inborn gesture.

The eyebrows are raised rapidly for one second and are dropped again in order to draw attention to the other person's face to exchange signals. It is not used in the Japanese culture since it can be interpreted as being impolite.

Looking up

When a woman lowers her head and looks up, it appeals to men since this is a submissive gesture. The men like this since the woman's eyes appear larger than they actually are and women often look more childlike. This is because a child will always look up at his parents while talking to them on account of being at a disadvantage with respect to height. This brings the parenting instinct in both men and women which would change the way a man looks at the woman.

Sideways Glance

You could use the sideways glance to show interest, hostility or uncertainty. When you combine this with a smile and slightly raised eyebrows, you will be showing interest. This gesture cluster is often used as a signal for courtship, especially by women. However, if the person were to combine this with downward eyebrows and an angry mouth, it would signal a critical or hostile attitude.

Blinking

A person who is not under stress or pressure would normally blink six to eight times in a minute. But, when a person is under pressure, he or she would blink rapidly. This is a gesture used by a person who is making an unconscious effort to block you from his sight for he may have become bored or feels he is superior to you. it would seem like their brain is unable to tolerate you any longer and cannot wait to remove you from their sight.

Tight Lipped Smile

The lips would form a straight line and conceal the teeth. This gesture sends a message that the person is withholding his or her opinion or is withholding some information which they would definitely not want to share with you. this gesture is more common in women since they would use it unconsciously when they dislike someone. Women can decipher this gesture within minutes while men are oblivious to this gesture.

Jaw Drop

This is a smile that needs to be practiced. The person will need to drop their lower jaw giving the people around them the impression that they are happy or in a playful mood. People like The Joker in Batman use this to ensure that their audience is happy.

Down Mouth

The opposite of a smile is to pull the corners of the mouth downward. This gesture or expression is used when a person is unhappy, angry, tense or depressed. If a person always holds negative thoughts in his mind, the corners of his or her mouth would settle into this position permanently leaving them with a permanent down mouth expression.

Chapter 9:
Common Gestures

We never think consciously about the gestures that we make on a regular basis or the non – verbal things that we do. For instance, when you hug a person and you are only given a pat on your back, you would probably assume that it is out of affection. However, it means that the other person wants to end the hug. If you are not keen on hugging someone but are being forced into doing it, you will probably begin to pat the air even before you have been pulled into the hug. This chapter lists out some common gestures that you may use often without your knowledge.

Head Nod

In many cultures, this gesture is used to signify agreement. The person will make a stunted bow with his head – he will bow his head down but will stop it short which results in a nod. This gesture is submissive since you are agreeing to go along with the other person's point. Research shows that people who were born blind, dumb and deaf use the same way to agree to a point, which concludes that the head nod is a submissive gesture that is inborn.

Head Shake

Research conducted on gestures also indicated that shaking the head from side to side, implying no, is an inborn gesture which could be the first gesture ever learned by human beings. The theory behind this is that a newborn baby shakes its head from side to side when it has had enough milk trying to reject its mother's breast.

When you find that someone is using a head shake with an affirmative sentence, you need to be skeptical about it. If a person says, "I can see what you are saying" and accompanies that sentence with a shake of his head, it implies that he is not entirely okay with the point.

Head Shrug

The head shrug which is pulling the head down while raising the shoulders helps in protecting the neck from any form of injury. This is a gesture that is always a part of a cluster – when you hear a loud bang or when you think somebody is about to hit you, you would make this gesture. When this gesture is made in a business or a personal context, this would be a submissive form of an apology, which would foul your plan to appear confident.

If a person walks past someone they consider superior, they would use this gesture which would give them away as a submissive. You will be able to identify the status between individuals using this gesture.

Picking Lint

If a person is not agreeable to the opinions and the attitudes of the people around him and he does not want to say anything about it, he would begin to pick up dust or lint from his clothing. He would be looking down at his clothing and away from the speaker. This is a common sign of disapproval and one would only use this when he does not like what is being said although he could be agreeing to what is being said.

Legs Spread Apart

This gesture is more prominent in men and is often seen performed by apes who are trying to establish a certain control and authority over the other apes. The ape would prevent the fight and would only want to look dominant. This is the same with men. They may perform this gesture unconsciously, but it does send a sense of authority to the people around him. If a man uses it in front of women in business, they are intimidating the woman because the woman cannot mirror this gesture.

Leg over Arm of Chair

This is a gesture that is performed often by men since it also uses the gesture above. It shows that the man has taken ownership of the chair and also signals an aggressive and informal attitude.

Straddling a Chair

Many centuries earlier, men used to use shields to protect themselves during war. If a person sits this way on a chair, it goes to say that the man is trying to protect himself from an attack of any kind.

Chapter 10:
The Body and Mind Connection

Most people say that the mind and the body are connected very deeply. People believe that the mind controls the actions of the body, but there is more to this than that. This chapter will help you understand the intricacies of the connection between the mind and the body.

How does the mind affect the body?

The mind and body have a connection that is not as elusive as people claim it is. The connection always exists for better or for worse. Let us look at a few examples for the same.

You may have noticed that your mouth waters when you think of your favorite food. When you are gearing up for an exam, interview or even a date, you have butterflies in your stomach. This goes to show how your thoughts have begun to affect your digestive system. If you see that an athlete has performed inefficiently during a game, it could be because of the fear that he has in his mind. He could have choked with fear because of which he may have lost the ability to control and coordinate his actions.

Every person experiences the mind and the body connection implying this is not something that only occurs at times. This connection is very real and because of it we do get into some tricky situations. For instance, when you do not like somebody, your brain automatically will detect and display an emotion of disgust or an emotion of anger depending on how you feel. This emotion is automatically displayed on your face and your body will send a signal to that person without you even realizing it.

Has there been a time when you were talking to someone and you had a very strong feeling that that person did not want to be there talking to you? If you take a picture of that very moment, you will see that the person is nodding at what you say and smiling and laughing wherever deemed necessary. However, when you look at his posture, you will find that his body is turned away from you, implying that he is looking for an exit. If you look carefully at the direction in which his body is facing, you will be able to gather which direction he would rather be going in.

When you have a meeting where you are talking to a person face – to – face, if the other person has decided to end or leave the conversation, he or she will turn their body and their feet and point towards the nearest exit. If you are a part of this conversation, you will need to make sure that you do something in order to grasp the person's attention again. Otherwise, you have to end the conversation on your own terms in order to maintain control over the conversation.

What do body angles say?

The distance that people maintain between each other when conversing gives a viewer an understanding of the degree of intimacy or interest. The angle at which a person may orient his or her body provides a non – verbal cue on their attitude towards the other person.

Open Positions

Animals generally signal to another animal when it comes to fighting with that animal. They will approach each other head on. If the other animal has accepted the challenge, it will signal in the very same way thereby reciprocating the challenge. However, if an animal does not want to fight but wants to observe the other animal, it will approach the animal sideways in order to check the animal out.

The same applies to human beings too. When a person addresses an audience with a strong attitude, while standing erect and facing the audience directly, is always perceived as an aggressive man. In contrast, a person who is addressing the audience while pointing his body a little away from the audience is considered a confident person and not aggressive.

In order to avoid coming off as an aggressive person, you will need to angle your body at 45 degrees when talking to another person to appear friendly. When you angle yourself at 45 degrees, the other person will automatically angle himself at 45 degrees thereby forming an angle of 90 degrees. If you are in confined spaces, like trains or elevators, you will be unable to angle your body at a 45 degree angle. In such situations, you will need to angle your head at that angle.

Closed Positions

When two people are intimate with each other their body angles will automatically change to 0 degrees from 45 degrees, implying that they directly face each other. If you want to monopolize a person's attention, you will need to use this position and other gestures while talking.

If a man were courting a woman, he would face that woman directly and close the distance between them thereby moving into her intimate space. If the woman accepts this, she will orient herself to face his body and allow the man to enter her personal space. When compared with the open position, the distance between people in the closed position is minimal.

In addition to displaying certain courtship gestures, the people in the conversation may also mirror each other's gestures and would continue to maintain eye contact if both of them were interested. However, this position can be used between people who are hostile towards each other and are gearing up for a challenge.

Research has shown that women fear attack from the back and are wary of anyone approaching them from the back while men fear attach from the front and are wary of anyone approaching them from the front. Make sure that you do not stand right in front of a man you have just met since his mind will perceive it as an aggressive signal.

If you are meeting a person for the first time, try to keep yourself in an open position. This will give the person's mind the signal that you are only trying to be friendly.

How do you control your thoughts?

When you are talking to someone new and you are not very comfortable with them, your body will send signals to him or her because of your thoughts. When you are interested in the person, you will begin to show some signals to that person because your mind will automatically direct your body to do so. In such situations, it is always good to make sure that you have a certain level of control on your mind.

1. If a person has invaded your personal space and you are not comfortable with it, you can slowly start angling your body to the open position to help you.

2. When you find that a person is angling away from you, it is a cue that the person is no longer interested in the conversation and it is best for you to try a new way to converse with the person.

3. If you are interested in the person and the other person has made it clear to you that he or she is interested too, you can slowly move into the closed position. Make sure that you do not rush into this position since that could scare the person off.

You need to remember that your mind is very strong when it comes to controlling your body. Your legs will always give you away even if you are controlling your gestures. Make sure that you face the person you are talking to, without angling yourself or your legs away from the person.

Chapter 11:
Rules for Accurate Reading

There are three rules that you must remember when it comes to reading body language to avoid making any errors.

Rule 1: Read gestures Together

A mistake that an amateur makes is to isolate a particular gesture and interpret it while forgetting to consider the circumstance and other gestures. For instance, when a person is scratching his or her head, it could mean many things – dandruff, fleas, lying, forgetfulness, uncertainty and sweating. This gesture would depend on many other gestures that may occur at the very same time.

Like every language, body language also has words that form sentences and punctuation. Every gesture performed is a word and each word may have multiple meanings. For instance, the word season has two meanings – it could mean to season your food or could be talking about the four seasons. If you assume it to be one of the meanings without paying heed to the conversation that was happening, you will have failed to grasp the central idea of the conversation. Another example for such a word would be dressing – it could mean your clothing or could also mean the salad dressing, or the act of putting clothes on or applying a medicine to a wound and so on.

It is only when you are able to put a word along with other words into a sentence that you will be able to grasp the meaning of the sentence fully. Gestures, like words, come in sentences or clusters which reveal the truth of a person's feelings or attitude. Like a verbal sentence, body language also needs three words to form a sentence which would define the feelings or the emotions of the person. A perceptive person will be able to read the sentences of body language and will also be able to accurately match this sentence with a verbal sentence.

You will always need to look at the clusters of gestures if you are looking at reading correctly. Every person has certain gestures that are repetitive which would imply that the person is feeling under pressure or is bored. When a person is twirling their hair or touching their hair repetitively, it could mean that the person is bored. But, when you isolate this gesture it could mean that the person could either be anxious or uncertain. People often stroke their head or their hair because their mother comforted them that way when they were children.

For instance, let us look at a gesture that people would perform when they are disinterested or unimpressed by what they are hearing.

The most important critical evaluation gesture is the hand- to –face. This is where the person points his index finger up his cheek while the other finger covers the mouth and the thumb is placed below the chin. The further evidence that he has a lot of critical thoughts is supported by the arm that is crossing the body while the legs are crossed tightly. This is a defensive gesture and could also mean that the person is hostile or negative towards the speaker. This would say something like, 'I do not like what is being said by you and I am trying to hold my negative feelings back.'

Rule 2: Look for Consistency

There is research that shows that non –verbal signals and gestures have a greater impact as opposed to verbal communication. When two people who are not congruent with each other, especially women, they only rely on the non – verbal messages and completely disregard any verbal content.

If you were the speaker and you were to ask the listener in the example above to give you his opinion about what you had just said, and if he said that he did disagree with you, his gestures and body language would be consistent with what he just said. This implies that the two would definitely match. If he did say that he agreed with what you were saying, he would be lying since his words would not be congruent with what his body language says.

If you see a politician speaking confidently to a large group of people with his arms folded tightly across his chest and his chin is down, which shows that he is defensive and hostile; would you believe what he is saying? Would you trust him when he said that he was receptive towards the ideas of the youth, would you trust him? What if he were to tell you that he is warm and he does indeed care for the people while he made rude gestures or was pointing fingers at the crowd? Would you trust him then?

Freud once reported that a patient was expressing how happy she was in her marriage while slipping her wedding ring on and off while speaking to Freud about happiness in general. He was aware of how significantly important this gesture was and was not surprised when problems began to surface in that patient's marriage.

Observing clusters and consistency between words and the body language are extremely important to understanding and interpreting the attitude of a person correctly.

Rule 3: Always understand the context

You have to make sure that you consider the context behind how the gestures are made or at the time in which they occur. For example, if a person is sitting at the bus terminal with his legs and arms tightly crossed and his chin is pressed towards his chest on a cold winters' day, it may most likely mean that the person is feeling cold and not being defensive. But, if the person used the very same gesture while sitting across you while you were telling him an idea, this would be interpreted correctly as a negative reaction towards your idea. You could probably imply or infer that he is going to reject your offer.

Why is it easy to misread?

If a person, especially a man has a weak or a limp handshake, he is considered to have a very weak character. You will learn over the course of the book on the different handshake techniques. But, if a person has arthritis in their hands, they will definitely have a softer handshake to avoid the pain as opposed to a strong handshake. Artists, surgeons, musicians and others who have an occupation that is delicate prefer not to shake hands with people. If they are forced to shake hands, they will just use a lame handshake in order to protect their hands.

A person who wears tight clothing or ill – fitting clothing would not be able to use certain gestures and this would affect their body language. For instance, a person who is obese will be unable to cross his or her legs. Women who wear very short skirts would cross their legs tightly in order to protect themselves. But, this can be misconstrued as them being inapproachable and people would shy away from asking them anything.

Such circumstances apply only to a minority of people, but it is extremely important certain physical restrictions or disabilities that a person may have in order to avoid misreading any gestures or movements made by that person.

Can a person fake it?

People often wonder if they can fake body language. The honest and general answer to this is no since there would be no consistency between the gestures made by you, along with the micro signals made by your body and the words spoken by you.

For instance, when you place open palms on your lap, it is associated with honesty. If a person is faking it, he would put his palms out and also smile at you while telling you the lie. But, his micro gestures would give him away - the corner of his mouth may twitch and his eyebrow may lift or his pupils may contract. This would mean that the person listening would not believe what the person is saying, women especially will not.

Conclusion

There are various aspects of body language that have been covered in this book. If you have read till this part of the book but could not remember everything, fret not. Below key points are all you will need to keep in mind when you are working on your body language.

Tips to keep your body language positive

- Always keep a relaxed posture irrespective of whether or not you are standing or sitting. Make sure that you keep you back straight and not stiff. When you keep your shoulders relaxed, you will find yourself comfortable and confident.

- Do not sprawl when you are sitting, but keep your legs slightly apart even when you are standing. This would give people the impression that you are at ease with yourself.

- Lean in towards the person speaking to you to give them the impression that you are listening intently to what they are saying to you. If you lean away, then you are demonstrating signs of disinterest or hostility.

- Do not cross your arms in front of your chest since that would turn the people away from you. Keep your hands hanging comfortably on your side and bring your arms together on your lap to show that you are open to talking.

- Always maintain eye contact with the person you are talking to. Do not stare at them, just look at them while talking and only look away from them occasionally.

When you maintain good eye contact, you are giving the person the impression that you are interested in them.

- Focus on slowing your speech. You have to take deep breaths and make a conscious effort to slow your speech down.

- Do not keep looking at the time when you are talking to a person. This would give them the notion that you are not interested in what they have to say to you. If you are in a hurry, be polite and let the person know about it.

- Never look at the ground while talking to a person since that would give them the feeling that you are disinterested and shy.

- Never stand too close to a person or invade his personal space since that would give him a negative feeling about you.

- Do not repeatedly touch your face since that would give the person an indication that you are lying.

- Do not tap your fingers or legs too much since that would give the person a sign of impatience which will not bode well with them. Let the person know that you are in a hurry earlier to avoid any negative effects.

Keep these points in mind when you are speaking to people around you. If you find that a person you are talking to is displaying negative body language, you will need to change tack to gather his attention.

Reading body language comes with practice. Try going to parks and observe people on how they react to the others around them. Always practice and keep certain key points in mind when you are communicating to others.

I hope you will find these body language guides useful and apply it well to your benefits. Nothing beats

www.ingramcontent.com/pod-product-compliance
Lightning Source LLC
Chambersburg PA
CBHW060219290526
45789CB00003B/1333